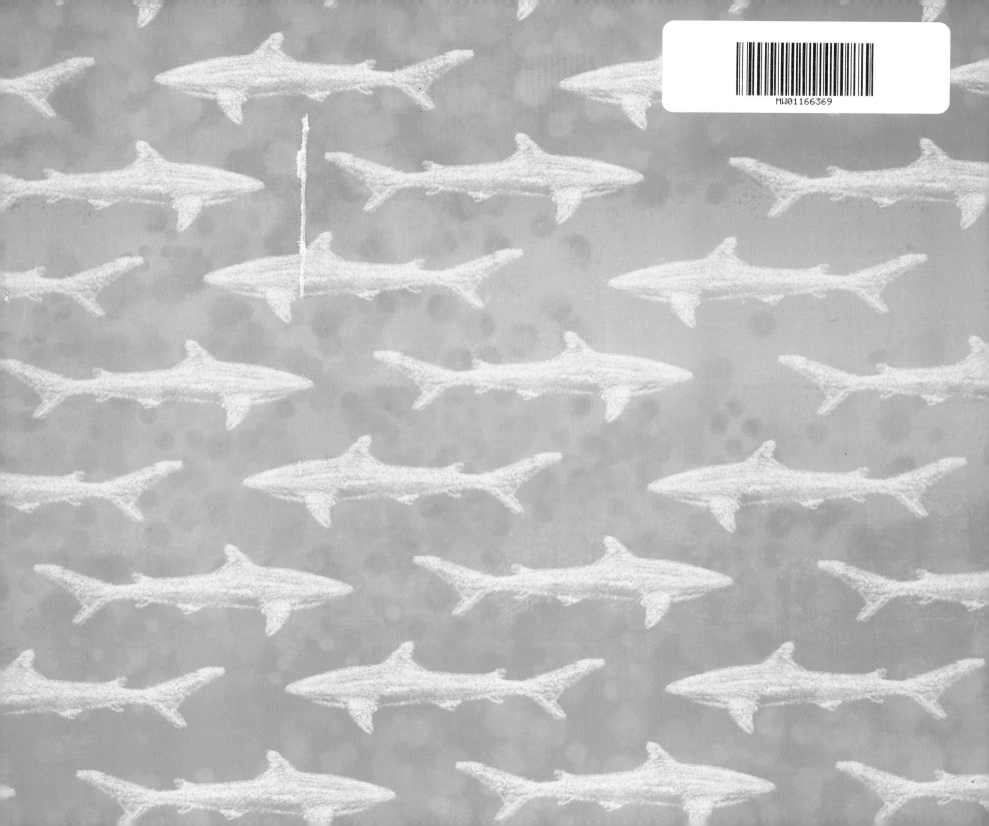

Beyond the white sandy beach,
  the foamy ripples,
  the rolling surf,
below the warm, crystalline water
  bathed in sunlight,
in an undersea world
  exploding with color,
slips a stealthy hunter,
  seeking,
  circling.
But without warning . . .

**She's HOOKED!**
Thrashing!
Rolling!
Diving!

**What will ease her pain?**

# SHARKS UNHOOKED

## THE ADVENTURES OF CRISTINA ZENATO, UNDERWATER RANGER

WRITTEN BY **PATRICIA NEWMAN**
ILLUSTRATED BY **BECCA HALL**

Ⅿ Millbrook Press / Minneapolis

Beyond the rocky beach,
the bubbly ripples,
the crashing surf
*Click! Pop! Fizz! Crackle!*
below the cold, clear water
swam a young Italian girl named Cristina.

Most of the year,
    Cristina lived in Africa
    in what was once Zaire
    while Papà Cesare helped build a railroad
    and Mamma Vanna worked in the office.
Cristina and her friends played with monkeys,
    tiptoed among snakes,
    and rescued rhinoceros beetles.
But she missed the sea.

Every summer, Cristina returned to her beloved ocean off the coast of Italy
   to glide with fish,
   free dive for shells,
   and snorkel above octopuses sending hatchlings out to sea.
She imagined becoming an underwater ranger,
   protecting the deep blue
   together with her shark friends.

She wanted to learn to scuba dive so she could breathe underwater.
But although Papà inspired Cristina to love the sea,
   he said scuba diving was too dangerous.

And Cristina only ever saw sharks in movies,
   never in the wild.
   Not once.

As Cristina grew up, she felt like
a fish out of water
among girls who preferred
clothes,
makeup,
hair,
boys.

Girls who didn't love the water
and never thought about making friends with sharks.

Sadness made her ill, and illness made her sad.
She felt restless as a teen,
    unsatisfied as a young adult.

After college, she visited the Bahamas,
home of sparkling water,
white sandy beaches
and, best of all,
scuba teachers.

The first time Cristina rolled off a boat into the open ocean
*Splash!*
warm water embraced her,
happy memories bubbled up,
peace surrounded her.

And then . . . she saw them.

"You have sharks?!"

Cristina made the Bahamas her home
and became an expert diver.
She marveled at sharks' strength and speed,
snouts that sense movement,
skin with tiny teeth-like scales for silent swimming.

She understood sharks' role as ocean guardians,
    feeding on the weak and the sick
    to control the number of fish in the sea
    and balance the food web.

Cristina and the sharks danced together—
    underwater rangers
    protecting the deep blue.

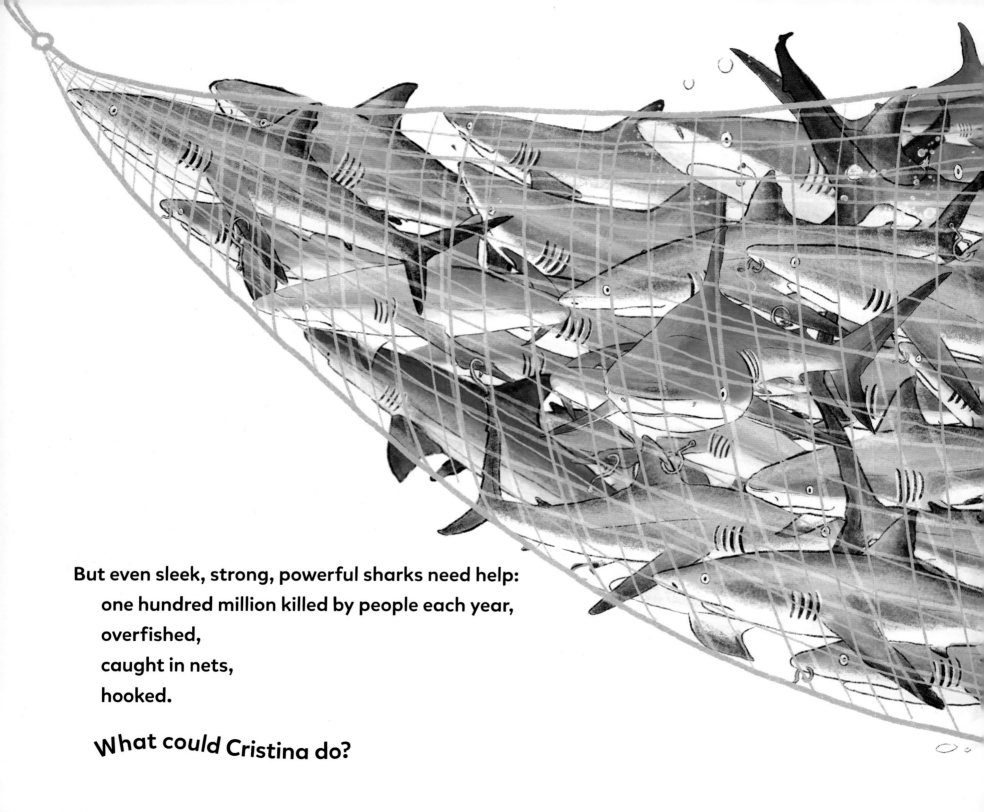

But even sleek, strong, powerful sharks need help:
    one hundred million killed by people each year,
    overfished,
    caught in nets,
    hooked.

What could Cristina do?

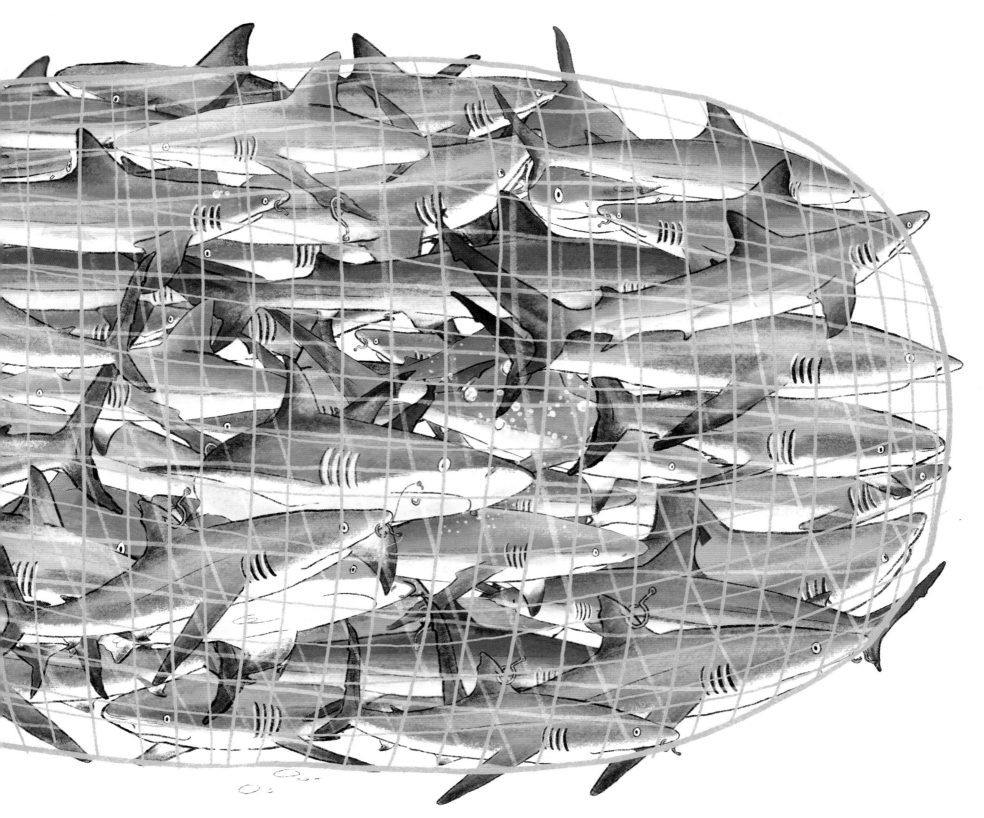

Down,
   down
   she dove,
   wrapped in a chain suit for protection,
   carrying mackerel treats to lure them closer.
A shiver of sharks silently loomed,
   some inquisitive,
   some bold,
   some shy.
Cristina rewarded calm behavior
   and slowly,
   slowly
   built trust.

Some returned so often Cristina named them:
> Foggy Eye,
> Stumpy,
> Grandma,
> Crook.

At long last, a shark glided into her lap,
> a gift she'd waited for her entire life.

One day, a wounded shark approached,
leery,
suffering.

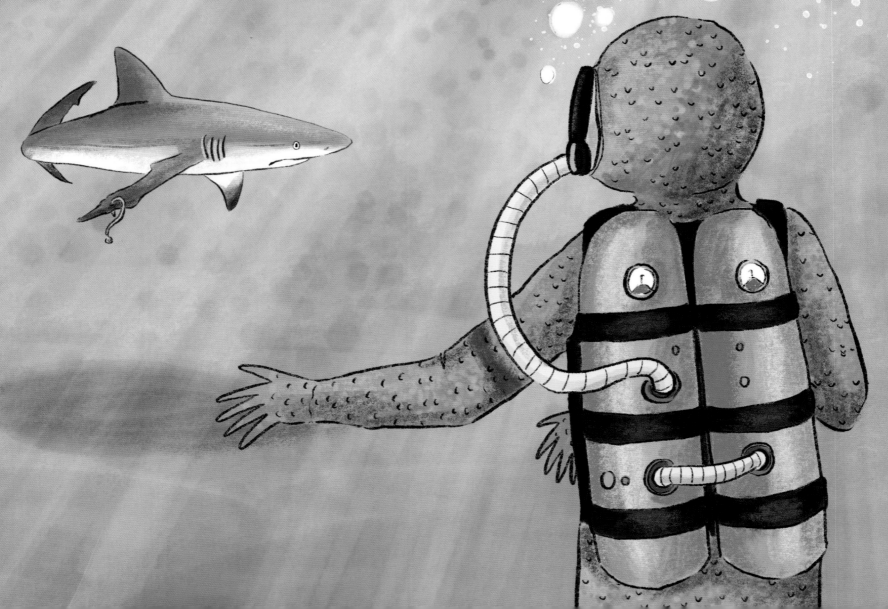

Cristina found her courage
and cautiously reached out.
**Snap!**
She removed a fishing hook from its fin.

After that, more sharks found Cristina
with hooks in their gills,
tails,
nostrils,
fins.
Did sharks share the news?
No one knows.

But with every hook, Cristina forged a bond
and felt more confident.

Then one day, Foggy Eye swam up to Cristina.

**Thrashing!**

**Rolling!**

**Diving!**

What would ease her pain?

In Cristina's lap, Foggy Eye finally calmed.
Cristina peeked into her mouth
and saw the hook deep in her throat.

Could Cristina do this?
Did she dare?
Had *anyone* ever dared?

When Cristina and the shark breathed as one,
she opened Foggy Eye's jaws,
ignored her rows of sharp teeth,
reached deep inside,
grabbed the hook,
and pulled.

Another shark, safe.

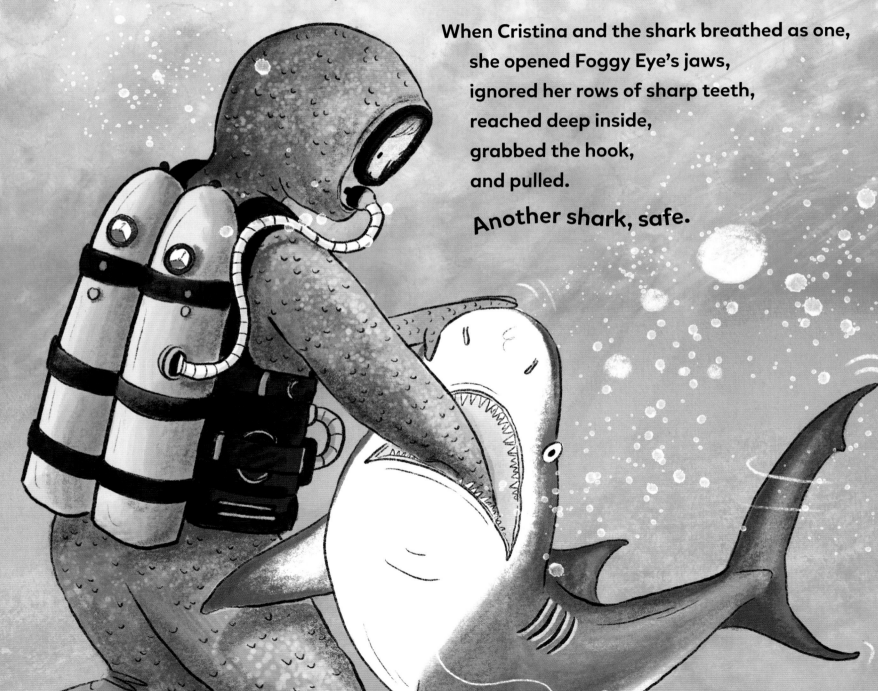

Over time, Cristina removed
   short hooks,
   long hooks,
   skinny hooks,
   fat hooks,
   shiny hooks,
   rusty hooks.

At first, she tossed them in the trash,
   but then she realized they had the power
   to hook humans—
      to make them listen,
      make them care about our guardians of the sea.

Beyond the white sandy beach,
the foamy ripples,
the rolling surf,
below the warm crystalline water
bathed in sunlight,
in an undersea world
exploding with color,
look for Cristina and her shark friends.
Underwater rangers
protecting the deep blue.

## OFF THE HOOK

Sharks protect the ocean by balancing food webs. They feed on sick and injured marine life to help control fish populations and keep a variety of ocean habitats healthy.

As sharks patrol the deep, they swim into fishers' longlines that may extend for miles and contain thousands of hooks. The fish caught on these lines are easy prey for sharks. But when the sharks bite the fish, they too, become hooked. Although sharks are strong enough to bite through the line and swim away, the hook remains embedded in their fins, gills, mouths, nostrils, or throats. Many sharks carry multiple hooks.

The carbon steel hooks that fishers prefer can remain attached to a shark for an average of two and a half years before they rust away. Stainless steel hooks remain in sharks for at least seven years and possibly for the life of the shark. Hooks stuck in a shark's fins, gills, or mouth may interfere with feeding, and hooks embedded inside sharks cause internal bleeding or infection.

Cristina has removed more than three hundred hooks from Caribbean reef, nurse, and blue sharks.

photo © Kewin Lorenzen

Cristina greets Grandma (*center*).

## BE A FRIEND TO SHARKS

- Pack a zero-waste school lunch. Eliminate plastic from your lunch box. Bring your drink and food in reusable containers. Pack fruits and vegetables that come in their own wrapper, such as apples, bananas, and carrots. Plastic trash often winds up in the ocean, where sharks and other animals mistake it for food.

- Do you eat seafood? Sometimes shark meat is mislabeled as flake, sea eel, whitefish, huss, and lemonfish. Ask your fish seller what kind of fish you're buying and how it was caught. Buy only fish caught in ways that don't harm the environment or endanger species.

- Read more books about sharks. Five of my favorites are listed in the "More Shark Books" section.

- Teach others about sharks and why it's important to protect them.

- Visit Cristina's YouTube channel to see her shark videos: www.youtube.com/@czunderwater/videos.

## DO NOT TRY THIS AT HOME!

Cristina Zenato wants people to broaden their understanding of sharks and discover just how many different kinds there are. "When people hear the word *shark*, I want them to hear endless possibilities," she says. "It's like hearing 'bird' and picturing [more than] an eagle."

Cristina spends a lot of time "sharking around." One of her dive students once estimated that Cristina has spent a total of four years of her life underwater. While "underwater ranger" jobs do exist, Cristina does not work for a Bahamian marine protected area. But much like official rangers, she studies shark behavior, educates people of all ages about sharks, and recommends ways to protect sharks and their habitat. She also gauges their energy levels, and gets to know them as individuals before reaching out to touch them. Cristina has dived and bonded with more than twenty species of shark, including great hammerhead, great white, blue, mako, whale, and tiger sharks. "It is their decision to come in. It is their decision to stay. It is their decision to go," she says. And she never takes the privilege for granted.

I wanted to write about Cristina because she dared to make her dream come true. She forged a special relationship with sharks, and now she speaks around the world to prove they are complex beings with brains, personalities, and gentle sides, not the vicious man-eaters so often portrayed in the media. "No animal is vicious or useless," she says. "Every animal has a role and a vital importance in the chain of nature."

photo © Kewin Lorenzen

Cristina removes a hook from one of her girls, as she calls them.

## NOTE FROM CRISTINA

photo © Kewin Lorenzen

I had a childhood dream of roaming the oceans as their guardian and having sharks for friends.

Little did I know that as an adult, through coincidences, choices, and opportunities, I would dedicate my life to following my dream and making it come true daily.

I love sharks; I have loved sharks since the first time I understood and appreciated their presence.

My dad taught me that "there are no monsters in the sea, only the ones we make up in our heads."

I made it my lifetime goal to explore sharks, to educate myself and others better about them, and to promote their conservation.

Thirty years later, the tides somewhat favor sharks and I am happy to say that I obtained their complete protection at home in the Bahamas, where I have lived and worked as an underwater explorer. There is still more work to do, so I won't stop because we need sharks more than they need us.

You can learn more about my love for sharks and more about my work at www.cristinazenato.com and through my nonprofit at www.pownonprofit.org.

## SOURCE NOTES

"You have sharks?!" Cristina Zenato, interview with the author, August, 3, 2021.

"When people hear . . . an eagle." Brooke Morton, "Catching Up with the Shark Whisperer: Cristina Zenato," *SportDiver*, March 10, 2017, accessed September 3, 2023, https://www.sportdiver.com /catching-up-with-shark-whisperer-cristina-zenato.

"It is their . . . decision to go." BBC, "Blue Planet Live: The Woman Who Hugs Sharks," Facebook, video, 2:06, March 25, 2019, https://fb.watch/7zNaxehy4B/.

"No animal is . . . chain of nature." "Cristina Zenato Shark Consultant & Trainer," YouTube video, 3:06, posted by Kovac Family AB YouTube Channel, February 17, 2017, https://youtu.be /QsSQh83gzl8?si=ha9-rFhBHxPfxxYz.

## MORE SHARK BOOKS

Flood, Joe. *Sharks: Nature's Perfect Hunter*. New York: First Second, 2018.

Jackson, Carlee. *Sharks: What Do Great Whites, Hammerheads, and Whale Sharks Get Up to All Day?* Illustrated by Chaaya Prabhat. New York: Neon Squid, 2022.

Keating, Jess. *Shark Lady: The True Story of How Eugenie Clark Became the Ocean's Most Fearless Scientist*. Illustrated by Marta Álvarez Miguéns. Naperville, IL: Sourcebooks Jabberwocky, 2017.

Markle, Sandra. *The Great Shark Rescue: Saving the Whale Sharks*. Minneapolis: Millbrook Press, 2020.

Williams, Lily. *If Sharks Disappeared*. New York: Roaring Brook, 2017.

Millbrook Press™
An imprint of Lerner Publishing Group, Inc.
241 First Avenue North
Minneapolis, MN 55401 USA

For reading levels and more information, look up this title at www.lernerbooks.com.

Photographs copyright © Kewin Lorenzen.

Designed by Emily Harris.
Main body text set in Mikado. Typeface provided by HVD Fonts.
The illustrations in this book were created with digital illustration.

**Library of Congress Cataloging-in-Publication Data**

Names: Newman, Patricia, 1958- author. | Hall, Becca, illustrator.
Title: Sharks unhooked : the adventures of Cristina Zenato, underwater ranger / written by Patricia Newman ;
    illustrated by Becca Hall.
Other titles: Adventures of Cristina Zenato, underwater ranger
Description: Minneapolis : Millbrook Press , [2025] | Includes bibliographical references. | Audience: Ages 5–10 |
    Audience: Grades 2–3 | Summary: "From the time Cristina Zenato was young, she loved the ocean and she loved
    sharks. She grew up to become an advocate for these incredible creatures, diving with them and removing
    fishing hooks from their bodies" –Provided by publisher.
Identifiers: LCCN 2024020110 (print) | LCCN 2024020111 (ebook) | ISBN 9798765627235 (lib. bdg.) |
    ISBN 9798765659151 (epub)
Subjects: LCSH: Sharks—Conservation—Juvenile literature. | Sharks—Behavior—Juvenile literature. | Zenato, Cristina.
Classification: LCC QL639.3 .N489 2025  (print) | LCC QL639.3  (ebook) | DDC 597.3—dc23/eng/20240510

LC record available at https://lccn.loc.gov/2024020110
LC ebook record available at https://lccn.loc.gov/2024020111

Manufactured in Guang Dong, China by Dream Colour Printing
1-1010940-52105-6/12/2024

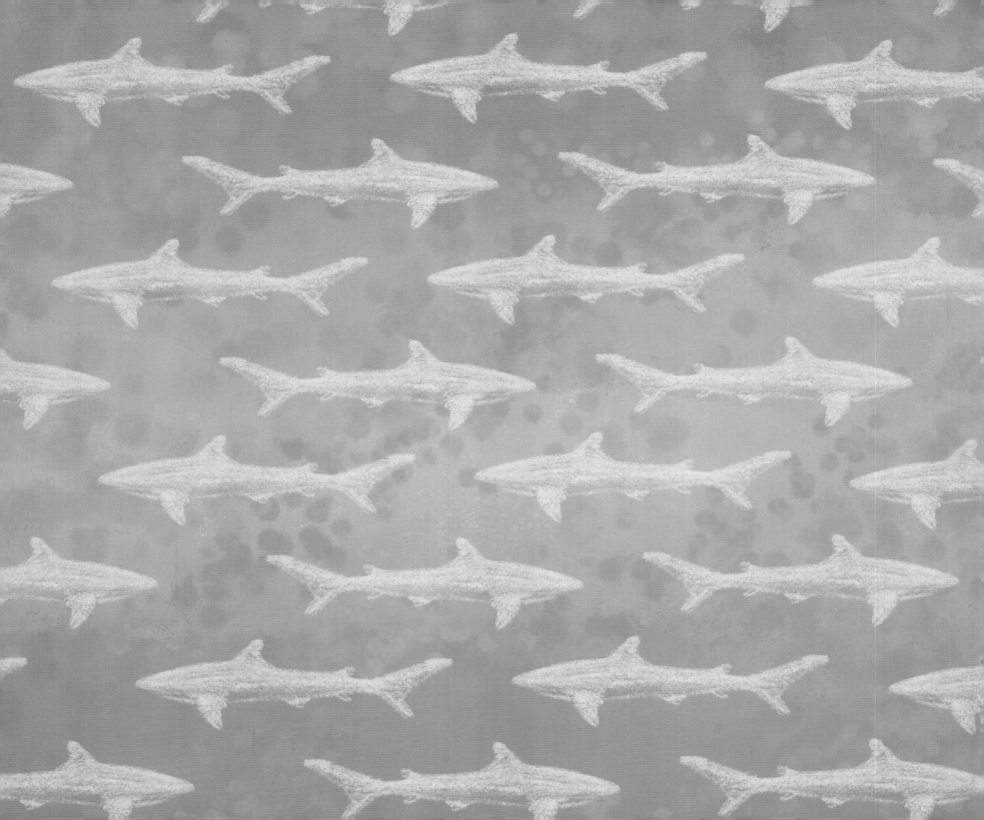